TIME FOR KIDS READERS

Life in the City

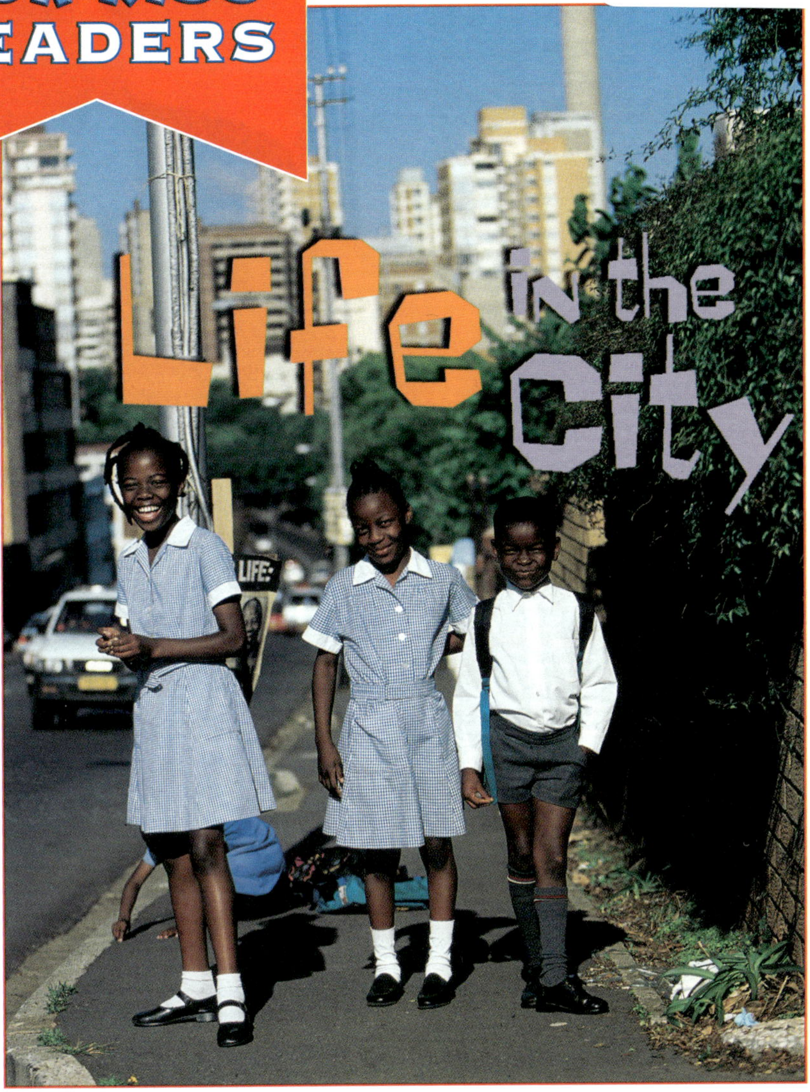

by Faith Adiele

Harcourt

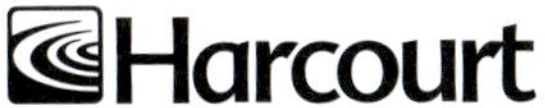

Orlando Austin Chicago New York Toronto London San Diego

Visit *The Learning Site!*
www.harcourtschool.com

A New Beginning

On August 26, 2000, a huge airplane landed at the airport in Abuja (ah•BU•ja), the capital of Nigeria (ny•JEER•ee•yuh), in Africa. The airplane was Air Force One, and it carried Bill Clinton, then President of the United States, and his daughter, Chelsea.

President Clinton had come to congratulate the lawmakers of Nigeria. Voters had elected them just 15 months earlier. When the elected officials took office in May 1999, they made history by forming Nigeria's first civilian government in almost 16 years. Since 1983 military men had ruled the country with an iron fist. And they had almost run Nigeria, Africa's most populous nation, into the ground. Now the nation of 127 million people was off to a new start. The government was determined to fix the damage that the military leaders had caused.

President Clinton reminded Nigerians that their nation was lucky. "Now at last you have your country back," he told the lawmakers, who were dressed in silky, colorful robes. The lawmakers represented the nation's many ethnic groups. "The hopeful fact," President Clinton said, "is that Nigeria's 250 different ethnic groups have stayed together in one nation." He urged Nigerians to avoid letting "the idea of one united Nigeria slip away."

Nigerian government officials welcome U.S. President Bill Clinton to their country.

No place in Nigeria illustrates Nigeria's problems and promise better than its former capital city, Lagos (LAY•gahs). Lagos is about 300 miles (about 480 km) southwest of Abuja, on Nigeria's coast. In 2002 about 14 million people lived on the city's four main islands and in its suburbs. The national government moved to Abuja in 1991 to escape the crowded conditions in Lagos.

Lagos is so big because it is a magnet for people from all over Nigeria. Most Lagosians, or people in Lagos, come from Nigeria's farming communities to look for work. Others come for the chance to study at the University of Lagos. Still others come looking for excitement. Lagos offers all three—and much, much more. The city shows how people from different ethnic groups can work and live together successfully. And so does Lagos State, the smallest of Nigeria's 36 states, in which the city of Lagos is located.

Where Wahala Rules

One thing the city of Lagos has a lot of, its residents say with a smile, is wahala (WAH•heh•la). In the language of the Yoruba (YAWR•uh•buh) people, *wahala* means "trouble." The Yoruba belong to one of Nigeria's three main tribes. They live in towns in the southwestern part of Nigeria, where Lagos is. Yorubaland, as the region is called, extends over the border into the neighboring country of Benin (buh•NEEN). Nigeria's second-largest tribe is the Hausa (HOW•suh). Hausaland covers most of northern Nigeria, spilling over into the nation of Niger (NY•jer). Most Hausa are deeply religious Muslims. The Igbo (IG•boh), members of the third-largest tribe, are mostly Christian. They are hard-working farmers who live in southeast Nigeria.

Wahala describes the hustle and bustle of Lagos perfectly. Traffic jams, crowded sidewalks, and lively outdoor markets give the city its character. So does a temperature that hovers around 90° F (32° C) all year long. Visitors say the sounds of Lagos are what they most remember. Lagosians speak many languages. In fact, practically every one of Nigeria's ethnic groups has its own language. But Nigeria's official language is English, enabling Nigerians from different backgrounds to understand one another.

Wahala also suggests the pressure a swelling population puts on services, such as water, electricity, phone service, and schools. Between 1990 and 2000, the population of Lagos grew by 30 percent. It was impossible during that short time to double water and electricity supplies and to double the number of schools and hospitals. And the newcomers keep coming. More than 30,000 people settle in Lagos every month!

During the dry season, from November to March, Lagosians must buy their water. But when the rainy season comes, from April to October, Lagos gets soaked. That can be a problem in a city that partly sits on four big islands. The highest place in Lagos is just 22 feet (about 6.7 m) above sea level.

Lagosians line up to get water. Sometimes the easiest way to carry a heavy bucket is on your head.

Traffic jams in Lagos are called "go slows."

Lagos's four main islands are Lagos, Iddo (ee•DOH), Ikoyi (ee•koh•YEE), and Victoria. A number of bridges connect these islands to the section of the city on the mainland. The city covers about 56 square miles (90 sq km).

Lagos Island is the heart of the city. The island is the nation's nerve center, the home of the nation's major businesses and factories. Big department stores, skyscrapers, banks, and oil companies—they're all here. And so are some of the offices of the state and national governments, all of which were once headquartered here. In the business districts, Lagosians are as likely to be wearing suits and ties as flowing, colorful robes and dresses.

Even though Abuja is the capital of Nigeria, Lagos is the nation's business center.

TFK Greetings from

Nigeria

English	Igbo	Yoruba	Hausa
Good morning	Ututu oma	E k'aro	Barka da safe
Good afternoon	Ehihie oma	E ka'san	Barka da yamma
Good evening	Anyasi oma	Eku'role	Barka da yamma
Good-bye	Ka emesia	Odabo	Sai an jima

A Trip to the Past

All four islands share a rich history. By the late 1400s, Lagos Island was home to Yoruba fishers and hunters. These people called the island Oko. Traders from the European nation of Portugal first visited the island in 1472. Over the next 200 years, Portuguese traders bought ivory and pepper from the Yoruba. In 1704, the island's chief gave the Portuguese the right to buy slaves as well. Soon Lagos Island became a major departure point for enslaved people. Ships carried them to North and South America. The slave trade continued until 1861, when Britain removed the Portuguese from Lagos and took over the islands.

The British ran Lagos as a colony, with a British governor in charge. On the mainland, Britain set up two larger colonies, Southern Nigeria and Northern Nigeria. (The name *Nigeria* comes from the Niger River, which runs through the nation.) In 1906 Lagos was made part of Southern Nigeria. In 1914 the British united the two remaining colonies. They made Lagos the capital of the new colony, which they called the Colony and Protectorate of Nigeria.

The colony became an independent nation in 1960. Lagos, a city of more than one million people, became the new nation's capital. Even then, Lagos was Nigeria's main business and manufacturing center. Nigerians began to flock there, hoping to find work. In 2002 Lagos was the world's sixth-largest city. By 2015 the city is expected to grow by about 10 million people, making it the third-largest city in the world.

Today, Lagosians rely on a number of industries for jobs. Many work in the shipping industry. Lagos has two main ports, one on Lagos Island, the other on the mainland. Lagos offers lots of factory work, too. Lagosian workers produce paint, soap, textiles, and cosmetics, among other things. They also assemble automobiles, radios, TVs, and other electronic devices. Many Lagosians make their living in the city's prosperous fishing industry. Millions work in the offices, where some of the nation's largest businesses are located. These include companies involved in Nigeria's major industry, the export of oil and natural gas.

Oil provides jobs for many Nigerians. Here, a worker checks pipes at an oil refinery.

"Africa's Most Thrilling City"

Nigerians move to Lagos not just for jobs but for excitement. One U.S. reporter called Lagos "Africa's most thrilling city." Most Nigerians would agree. Many of Nigeria's—and Africa's—best artists, musicians, and writers live here. Lagos is Nigeria's media center, home to the nation's television industry and at least a dozen newspapers. Since 1999, those newspapers have been free to print what they want. When the military was in charge, it was a crime to criticize the government.

Thousands of tourists visit Lagos every year simply to listen to its music. One popular musical form is called Afrobeat. Afrobeat is a mix of African melodies and rhythms with American jazz and soul music thrown in. The creator of Afrobeat, Fela Anikulapo-Kuti (feh•LA an•ee•koo•LA•po koo•TEE), died in 1997. But his musician son, Femi, is a master of the form. Crowds gather at his club on the mainland every night to listen and dance to his music.

Juju (JOO•joo) is another type of music that Nigerians love. Juju features complicated guitar music and singing in harmony. But its main element is the "talking drums" of the Yoruba. In earlier times Yoruba drummers would tap out messages on these drums. Now the tapping simply adds to the beat of the music. One of the most famous juju musicians is King Sunny Ade (ah•DAY), who like Femi Kuti owns a nightclub on the mainland.

Lagos isn't all music. Far from it. The city's history and geography shape life there, and they have given visitors many opportunities for fun. Lagos has several relaxing beaches. The most popular is Bar Beach, on the southern end of Victoria Island. Other popular spots are Lekki (leh•KEE) Beach and Tarkwa Beach.

Fela Anikulapo-Kuti is the musician who invented Afrobeat, which is a popular form of music in Lagos.

Most residents of Lagos shop at outdoor markets. You can buy most things there—from food to clothes to artwork.

To get to the farthest beaches, Lagosians take a half-hour ride in water taxis. The taxis glide through the port and across the Lagos Lagoon, the body of water between the islands and the mainland. A bonus is the view taxi passengers get of some picturesque fishing villages.

The city's outdoor markets are a must-see for visitors. They sell just about anything you can imagine. The Balogun Market is so large that shoppers can get lost in its maze of passageways. Souvenir hunters love the Jankara (jon•KA•rah) Market, where they can find tie-dyed and indigo cloth, CDs of popular Nigerian music, wood carvings, and beads. Other markets on Lagos Island burst with goods. They sell everything from okra and yams to leather goods. The food stalls sell a lot of spices, tomatoes, and rice. These are the main ingredients of jambalaya (juhm•buh•LY•uh), a dish found at just about every West African celebration. East of Victoria Island, which Lagosians call "V.I.," are two amazing markets. Called Morocco 1 and Morocco 2, they're open only during the evening. Lagosians stop by after work or go there after dinner on family outings.

History on Parade

Nigeria's history is on display throughout Lagos. At the National Museum, visitors can marvel at the artifacts of ancient Nigerian civilizations. Some of these are small bronze statues from the kingdom of Benin. From the 1300s to the late 1800s, the obas (oh•BAHZ), or kings, had sculptors make small statues to honor them. Many of these Benin bronzes are on display at the museum. The museum also houses traditional musical instruments, costumes, masks, and wooden and ivory sculptures. A favorite of museum visitors is a pair of tiny wooden statues of twins. The Yoruba believe that twins bring good luck to their parents. Statues of twins are thought to bring good luck to their owners.

Visit the craft shop at the National Museum, and you can watch Yoruba women make adire (ah•dy•REH) cloth. Adire cloth is made from cotton dyed deep blue with indigo, a natural dye. Adire makers tie-dye, paint, or stencil unusual patterns on the cloth. Stop by the museum's restaurant for another treat—soups made from yams, peppers, and ground nuts. (Visitors hungry for hamburgers can buy them at a restaurant on Ikoyi. The restaurant is called New Yorkers.)

Not far from the National Museum is the city's biggest plaza, Tafawa Balewa (ta•fa•WAH bal•lay•WAH) Square. The plaza is at one end of Lagos Island's main avenue, Broad Street. The plaza was named for the man who led Nigeria to independence in 1960. Balewa remained head

of Nigeria's government until 1966. He was killed that year when Nigeria's army took over the government. The plaza used to be a racetrack. Except for the huge statues of horses, no one would know that today. The stables are now gone. These days, Tafawa Balewa Square is bordered with shops, office buildings, and restaurants.

A statue of Madam Tinubu has a place of honor in Tinubu Square.

About a mile and a half up Broad Street from Tafawa Balewa Square is Tinubu (tin•OO•boo) Square. This square is named after the Yoruba woman who in the 1800s donated the land the square is on. This square is at the very center of Lagos's business district. Christ Church Cathedral, built by the British in 1925, is nearby. The city's Central Mosque, the main Muslim place of worship in Lagos, is about a mile to the north.

The National Museum is filled with artifacts such as this bronze statue.

Obas and Super Eagles

Not far from Tinubu Square is an interesting reminder of Lagos's past links to Portugal. The buildings in this area don't seem very African. They have arched windows and doors, and fancy metal fences surround them. The neighborhood almost seems as if it had been brought in one piece from South America. In a sense it was. This area is called the Brazilian Quarter. It was built by former slaves. They had worked for years in the Portuguese colony of Brazil. Somehow they managed to get back to Africa, where they built a neighborhood of Brazilian-style homes. Today the buildings house shops, offices, and restaurants.

Another reminder of the city's past sits near the northern tip of Lagos Island. This is the Oba's Palace, the home of Lagos's traditional chief. Lagos still has an oba, although he no longer has much power. But he does have a house where the obas of Lagos have lived since 1670. With the approval of the oba's personal secretary, visitors can tour the palace.

One of the most popular areas to visit in Lagos is the Brazilian Quarter.

Celebrations and festivals take place throughout the year. Many honor local leaders.

Fans get a big kick from watching soccer matches. Soccer is Nigeria's favorite sport.

Lagosians are great sports fans, as anyone can tell from a single visit to the National Stadium on the mainland. Almost every Lagosian can rattle off facts about the national soccer team, the Super Eagles. People will tell you that the team is the best in the world—even when it loses. That's not a problem, though. From 1981 to 2000, the home team never lost a game at the National Stadium.

That's the kind of record that makes Lagosians smile. They like to win at whatever they do. The license plates on automobiles registered in Lagos carry the motto *Centre of Excellence*. Much of Lagos, though, isn't excellent. The phone service is unreliable. The water system often fails to deliver water. The wires don't always deliver electricity. But there is a lot that is excellent about the Lagosians themselves. They are skilled workers and they work hard. Every year, Lagosians produce more goods and services than the people of most other African nations.

Skilled workers float lumber to season it before it is cut into boards.

U.S. President Bill Clinton wears a traditional Nigerian outfit as he greets people. Loose-fitting clothes keep people cool in Nigeria's tropical climate.

TFK FAST FACTS

6 Most Populated Cities in the World

Tokyo, Japan
Mexico City, Mexico
Mumbai (Bombay), India
Sâo Paulo, Brazil
New York City, New York, USA
Lagos, Nigeria

On his visit to Nigeria, President Clinton said, "You have beaten [the] odds to get this far." He was speaking to the country's leaders. But the same words could also be said to all Nigerians who have helped turn the country into a democracy.